THE RIVER

Originally from a farm in the west of Ireland, **Jane Clarke** now lives in Co. Wicklow. She holds a BA in English and Philosophy from Trinity College, Dublin and an MPhil in Writing from the University of South Wales. She has a background in psychoanalytic psychotherapy and combines writing with her work as a management consultant in not-for-profit organisations.

She received the Listowel Writers' Week Poetry Collection Prize in 2014 and her other awards include the Trocaire/ Poetry Ireland Competition (2014), Poems for Patience (2013), iYeats (2010), and Listowel Writers' Week (2007). Her poems have been published in *The Irish Times* and *The Irish Independent*, and by many journals, magazines, anthologies and websites. Her first collection, *The River*, was published by Bloodaxe Books in 2015, and was shortlisted for the Royal Society of Literature's Ondaatje Prize, given for a distinguished work of fiction, non-fiction or poetry evoking the spirit of a place. She also won the 2016 Hennessy Literary Award for Emerging Poetry with three poems from The River, 'For Isobel' 'Blue Bible' and 'Every Tree', as well as the inaugural Listowel Writers' Week Irish Poem of the Year in the Irish Book Awards 2016 for a later poem, 'In Glasnevin'.

www.janeclarkepoetry.ie

JANE CLARKE

THE RIVER

BLOODAXE BOOKS

ISBN: 978 1 78037 253 2

First published 2015 by
Bloodaxe Books Ltd,
Eastburn,
South Park,
Hexham,
Northumberland NE46 1BS.

Reprinted 2015 (twice), 2018

www.bloodaxebooks.com
For further information about Bloodaxe titles
please visit our website or write to
the above address for a catalogue.

Supported using public funding by
**ARTS COUNCIL
ENGLAND**

Cover design: Neil Astley & Pamela Robertson-Pearce.

Printed in Great Britain by Bell & Bain Limited, Glasgow, Scotland, on
acid-free paper sourced from mills with FSC chain of custody certification.

For Isobel

CONTENTS

We cannot step twice into the same river, nor touch mortal substance twice in the same condition. By the speed of its change, it scatters and gathers again.

HERACLITUS OF EPHESUS (530-470 BC)

Honey

Away, away, he shouts, sending her up the hill,
through furze and bracken, to gather sheep.
She snakes towards them, belly close to the ground,
listening for his whistle to bear left or right.

They raise their heads, sniff, ears pricked,
then flock together and run for the gate.
She comes back panting to stand at his side,
eyes bright, tongue lolling.

She had the herding instinct from birth;
when she was just a pup he'd find her
in the haggard rounding up the hens.
You'll make a right cod of her, he gives out,

when the children dress her up like their teacher
in their mother's headscarf and glasses.
They sit her on a chair at the kitchen table,
offer her a cup of tea and a scone.

A Sunday close to lambing, three men in the yard,
one with a shotgun under his arm. *Your dog and Dunne's
wreaked havoc last night, thirty ewes dead or dying,
mangled in barbed wire, lamb-beds hanging out.*

From an upstairs window they watch him
walk to the shed. He drags her by the scruff,
leaves her at their feet. He says nothing
when he comes in, says little for weeks.

Daily Bread

A white mist rises as she sifts a pound of flour
into the worn, tin basin, wide as Lough Corrib.

Blue veins lie like rivers on the map of her hands.
She measures one teaspoon of bread soda,

two teaspoons of salt. The plait at the nape
of her neck: a fisherman's rope coiled at the quay.

She scoops a hollow, pours a pint of buttermilk,
splashing and spluttering into the well.

With the rhythm of a rower she kneads rough dough
on the flour-dusted table, pushing it away,

pulling it back, pushing it away again.
With her wrist she flicks a lock, silver-grey frost

in December, from her high cheek bones. Readying
the bread for its hot harbour, she cuts a deep cross.

Rhode Island Reds

Haughty empresses of the byroad,
they scratch for grubs and worms
among dock and silverweed.

Back and forth they jerk their crowns,
precisely splaying one wrinkled
yellow foot before the other.

With flamenco flounces
they settle in dried-up puddles,
flick dust through their wings.

I remember the first time
I saw my mother choose one
and with deft wrist, wring its neck.

That night she plumped my pillows,
smoothed my sheets,
stroked the hair from my brow.

Harness Room

I have always loved this room under the loft,
between the cow house and stable,
though I don't know why. Is it the swallow's nest
in the rafters among cobwebbed hayforks,
bridle and saddle, slane and sickle?

The wire-meshed sunlight on lime-washed walls,
slash hooks and scythes, the rusted biscuit tins
of clout and stud nails on a sagging shelf
with a curry comb and a broken bicycle chain?
Is it the smells of grease and oil, petrol and paint,

the slab stone floor, softened by layers of dirt
and dust, where they'd hitch two cart horses
to the binder, a pony to the trap?
Is it a love for the naming of things; the clippers
and shears, the grape and the rake stacked at the hearth

with shovels and spades, crowbar,
sledgehammer, handsaw, band saw and axe?
Is it the tattered coat on a hook by the half-door,
the bucket of beastings, infra-red lamp,
the can of crimson paint and C-shaped brand

for the furrowed skin of newborn lambs? Or is it
because here's where we'd find him when my mother
sent us to call him for his tea; at the workbench he made
from creosoted railway sleepers, strewn with rasp, file
and whetstone, vice-grip, chisel and wrench?

The Blue Bible

Before breakfast we'd kneel
on the kitchen tiles for prayers,

then listen to our father
read a lesson from the blue bible

with sticking plaster along its spine,
a picture beside each story.

We took turns to choose:
the Good Samaritan,

Zacchaeus in the sycamore tree,
the loaves and fishes that grew

and grew to feed the multitudes.
Stories for people who worked the soil,

who watched over flocks of sheep.
We knew those people,

we knew the rain that ruined crops,
the seed that fell on stony ground,

the days when hope,
like a restless heifer, goes astray.

The Globe

My father had spun it thirty years before
        in the one-roomed schoolhouse down the road,

where pupils brought a sod of turf
        for the fire each day

and there weren't enough desks
        so the boys took turns to stand at the back.

Now faded to ginger, it rests on the master's table
        under the Easter Proclamation.

We vie for turns to search
        for Rhodesia, Ceylon, Abyssinia, Siam,

where missionaries from the parish
        have gone to save souls.

The master peers over his glasses,
        places the globe in my hands, like a chalice –

Take this to Mr Glennon's room.
        Proud as a dog with two tails,

I lift it chest-high,
        turn to my brother with a smile;

it falls – bare wooden boards,
        a crack, a hush, a broken world rolls.

The Suck

Sometimes together, most often alone,
we'd slip the catch on the rusted chain,
follow the cart track through the bottoms;
the river held our stories, it was where

we'd go to talk or cry or be quiet
in the company of the current,
whether it flowed fast after a flood,
rolled in circling eddies or drifted

smooth and slow past stands of alder
and silver-green willow. We could look
as far as the next bend or out to the island,
speckled with yellow iris, bordered with sedge.

We could dream of leaving, making lives
of our own, ask the river to bless us, let us go.

Dressage

You'll find your seat by riding
without saddle or reins,
sit deep, fall off, get on again.

Give and take with lightness
of hand and leg, shift your weight
as you feel how she needs to move.

You'll find your rhythm by listening
to the sequence of hoofs,
count aloud the beat of every stride.

Learn to read how she holds her head;
when to steady,
when to ask her to lengthen her pace

so the moment between lifting and falling
is held, sometimes so long
that together you don't touch the ground.

Against the flow

One day you knew you must turn,
begin to swim against the current,

leave the estuary waters, brackish
with sediment, head upstream

through riffles and deeps,
millraces that churn in spate,

over sheets of granite, across weirs,
into rapids that thunder-pound,

squeeze between boulders
to the upper reaches of the river,

those waters of blanket-bog brown,
where you'd find a place in gravel and silt

to hollow a dip,
to spawn a life of your own.

Dry Stone Wall

I'll skim the scraw, dig a trench
wide and deep to hold the given stone,

lay silver-grey against green, rocks
with square planes to build off,

slivers, thin as slate, to level in between.
I'll lift the stones, test where they'll nestle

into what's already there, fill the middle
with spalls, keep the edge stones

from falling in. I'll use old stones, dappled
with lichen and moss, leave gaps

to let the wind blow through, nooks
for pennywort and hart's tongue to grow.

I'll cover the joins, mind the batter, stack
each course till it takes its place between two fields,

keep a few of the finest for the finish,
long and flat capstones to span the width.

Dropping Slow

Afterwards we lie still,
your breath soft

across my forehead, mine
hot in the shallows

of your neck; bales of hay
stacked high, drying

in the sun, hens resting
on their roost

at the end of the day,
morning cobwebs

listening
on a hazel hedge.

Epithalamium

Love carves a path through fissures,
cavities, clay and shale,
like an underground stream,

flows over beds of mineral gems,
feeds hidden lakes, artesian wells,
tumbles out from the side of a hill

to run headlong over gravel,
open a channel down to the river
where waters from rills and creeks

mingle in the pull of the current,
promise to carry each other
until the river reaches the sea.

Vows

I can't promise it's chiselled from gold
in spirals that speak of forever.

I can't tell you it's wise as a mountain
with pines that reach for heaven.

I can't promise it's flawless as honey
gathered by bees in bell heather.

I can't say it's simple as silk
spun from cocoon into treasure.

But I promise it's rooted as rowan
with berries that sing to September.

I promise its to and its fro
will surprise like Glenmalure weather,

a seasoned row boat,
moored or unmoored at your pleasure.

Blue Ridge Trail

Through jewelweed and speedwell,
we leave the hemlock shade
where the trail meets Trout Lake.

Bluegill leap for caddis flies,
bullfrogs bellow in sedge,
swallows loop so low

their blue-black wings seem
to stroke the water before spiralling
upwards past the fiddler on a bench.

You watch and listen for every note
as if it's your father playing Schubert
in the kitchen, but here the old man

plays bluegrass, tapping his foot
to ballads that sing of railroad tracks,
lonesome as the last of the light.

For Isobel

I

Your father's alive in our house;
his books talk to ours on the shelves.

His photograph above the piano,
violin tucked under his chin.

You play the pieces he arranged,
quote his sayings and stories,

read his fountain-penned notebook
of favourite poems, Yeats,

Frost and Verlaine, for what
they tell about him.

You would run to keep up
as he walked Three Rock Mountain,

insisting you listen to the latest
from Sartre and Teilhard de Chardin.

Read to me from the Russians, he'd say,
those months when he lay in the Mater.

You cycled from your summer job,
grateful for each day and even

for his request through a medicated blur,
speak clearly and enunciate your words.

II

In a room full of strangers you sit by her side;
she plays with your fingers, fidgets with rosary beads.

She whispers meanderings of mama and dada
back home in Rockcorry and frets about the cows

that broke into the meadow, the stove to be blackened,
feeding corn to the goose, walking her brothers to school.

One day she shouts, you let her slap your hand.
The next she holds onto you. She cries when you leave.

She's forgotten your name, sees her sister in your face.
She's floating away from you, a leaf in a slow stream.

Today she smiles, looks you straight in the eye:
Agh Isobel, you're here. Where have you been?

When I knew

Because you cannot think of a better
way to pass the quiet time, you ask me
when I knew. I can hardly remember –
was it a bolt from the blue discovery,

like finding a rowan in the forest
thrown backwards in an out of season storm,
roots loosened, buds opening, its latticed
branches spread wide, leaves ready to unfurl,

or was it how celandines, violets,
columbine, buttercups and sorrel
find their way into a neglected space

without any fanfare, going unnoticed
until one morning after a quarrel
they seem to be calling, calling your name?

White Fields

Stopping by his jacket
on a hook at the end of the dresser,
she breathes him in,

cigarettes, silage and Brylcreem.
She touches rough tweed,
worn collar and cuffs,

pocketed coins, hay seeds
and the cold steel
of his bone-handled penknife.

She recalls mornings in fields
white with hoar frost, when the heat
between them would thaw the frozen pond.

He'd cut dark twine, shake out bales
in slivers of warmth for breathing clouds
of Friesians, circled round, waiting.

When the children came, he stayed longer
outside, always a lamb or a calf to mind,
a fallen wall that needed him.

Who owns the field?

Is it the one who is named in the deeds
whose hands never touched the clay
or is it the one who gathers the sheaves

takes a scythe to the thistles, plants the beech,
digs out the dockweed, lays the live hazel?
Is it the one who is named in the deeds

or the one who pulls ragwort on his knees,
lifts rocks into a cart, splits larch for stakes,
the one who gathers the sheaves,

slashhooks the briars, scatters the seed,
cuts his hand on barbed wire, hangs the gate?
Is it the one who is named in the deeds

or the one who could surely lead
to where children made a hiding place
in an old lime tree. He gathers the sheaves.

Is it the one who tends cattle and sheep,
and can tell you how the field got its name?
Is it the one who is named in the deeds
or the one who gathers the sheaves?

Before the war

these hills were peopled with trees,
everywhere, grey olive groves
stood old and gnarled as history,

sending silver-leafed branches
wandering wide and low
through the lives of those

who measured their wealth
in oil, crossed a friend's
threshold with oil, blessed

their children with oil,
who set the orchards singing
with the crack of sticks

on winter branches, plop of fruit
falling to blankets, laughter of girls
holding baskets, balanced and full.

Lighthouse Keeper

It's twenty years now since they unmanned the lantern,
left it unwatched and sent me away,
yet often I dream of that broad beam of light
sweeping the white caps, combing the waves.

Some summer's day take the ferry to Clare Island,
see a black and white tower overlooking Clew Bay,
where I first heard my mother say the rosary for sailors,
watched her fry herring on the wood-burning stove.

Where myself and my father cleaned rain-battered windows,
polished brass instruments until they gleamed like stars,
peered through the telescope at kittiwakes and guillemots,
searched for the Seven Sisters in dark, winter skies.

These landlocked days I'm washed up like wreckage
and all I could wish for is tussocks of sea pinks,
grey seals sleeping on rocks pummelled smooth,
echoes of footsteps on spiral stone stairs.

The Catch

It was dusk, the grass still held the heat
of the day when the moth man left a box
under the honeysuckle in my garden.

Through the night his lantern dazzled
cinnabars, orange swifts, brindled beauties,
drew swallowtails and moon moths to the trap.

Soon after dawn I crept barefoot
to watch the catch, their hindwings tucked
beneath forewings, asleep. One by one

I lifted them, studied their colour and camouflage
until warmed by my hands, their wings
began to quiver, waking to the strangeness of day.

Every life

She fills the days with movement, cuts back
on coffee and wine, eats blueberries, red peppers,
broccoli, kale, writes down the words she won't
let herself say, like arid, fallow, barren, ache.

The man on the radio says every life is laced
with loss, that's what makes us whole. She reads
a book about Buddhism to learn how not to
want, adds to the list of places it's best to stay

away from; supermarkets, coffee shops, beaches,
hospitals, parks. She pretends the temperature charts
haven't taken the pleasure away, stops herself
thinking of names, Oisín, Molly, Sinéad,

won't let herself hope when she's a few days late,
lists her consolations and tries to avoid the questions,
like how did this happen to them, what was it they did
or didn't do, how will they know when it's time to stop.

River at Dawn

The Shannon moves through morning mist
under the arches of Banagher Bridge,
steady and slow as a draught horse in harness.

A row boat skims the surface with a whisper;
eight oarsmen focused on the sweep
they must deliver to the coxswain's call,

lean in, catch, pull back, release.
Past reed beds, yellow with loosestrife,
they feather their blades, drops fall in unison

from the spoon of every oar. A heron flies up
from the callows, leads river and rowers
into the day, lean in, catch, pull back, release.

callows: flat grassland alongside rivers that flood in winter

The Fisherman

he stands in the shallows
        at dusk   silk and feather fly tied

a fish on the rise   swish of line
        cast upstream beyond the reeds

and fallen beech   rod flexed
        water churning

line taut as a fiddle string
        he spools it out   little

by little   rod-tip held high
        lets the fish run

until it charges full tilt
        bursts up through rush of foam

twisting turning
        head and tail flailing

bronze-flecked trout ready
        for beheading and gutting

but he lays out his catch
        on the bank   loosens the hook

slips it back to the Suck
        quiet as flaggers

flaggers: yellow flag iris

The Suitcase

As children they didn't understand
that despair was a neighbour
of love and if you were lucky
it stayed beyond the garden gate,
just visiting from time to time
to borrow sugar, test faith.

As children they didn't understand
that when their mother showed them
the nightie, toothbrush, nylons,
miniature bible and summer dress
she kept packed in the suitcase
under the bed, it was herself

she was telling, I can go, if I want to.
Sometimes they checked
had she emptied it yet, sometimes
they wanted to shout, go if you're going,
why wait? They didn't understand
it was the suitcase that helped her to stay.

Inheritance

I'd give it all up in a minute,
every last rock,
stream and sod of it.

They can have the price of sheep,
the grant for the cattle shed,
and the bills from the vet.

They can have himself
with his humours and stories
and fear of anything new.

They can have the saplings
planted last spring, the kestrels
nesting in the mill.

I swear I wouldn't miss a thing,
not one swallow swooping
through the yard, not the geese

on the callows in March,
not one blade of foxtail
or meadow-grass heavy with dew.

For Michael

Despite the fire
of the rowan berries,

sedums' copper glow,
our garden is fading.

Nights grow colder
and we are waiting:

phone calls about your eating,
emails about your sleeping,

texts about your breathing.
We rake leaves,

cover dahlias with straw,
gather fallen apples.

In the waning light
we wheel one barrow after another.

Let there be

From breath to breath
from dusk to dusk

let there be rainfall
when the soil is parched as rock

let there be sunshine
when the barley bends to be cut

let there be rainbows
when the days are short of light

let there be wind
when our boats are turned for home.

Broken

Piebald and skewbald,
bred to pull heavy loads,

they've lived tethered
by bridle and ropes.

Thickset as boulders,
heads hanging low,

they wind a serpentine path
to the barbed wire fence,

where they reach
for rolled barley, crushed oats.

A blustery wind sets them bucking,
whinnying like colts;

they dig in front hooves,
toss their heads skywards,

kick up fetlocks,
break into a gallop, unfettered.

The Ringer

It was my mother taught me to watch
blood-breasted stonechats on a barbed-wire fence,

to listen for the mournful song of a linnet,
a meadow pipit's pseeping alarm.

I couldn't count how many I've caught,
ringed, sexed, measured and weighed

but I'll always remember the first time
in the woods beyond Skibbereen,

when I opened a mist net at dawn,
held a goldcrest hammocked between

finger and thumb, a rosebud in my palm.
Olive nape, yellow crown, eyes

black and glistening as Kilkenny marble.
I held my breath, lest I harm her,

turned my hand so she lay on her back.
She settled as if lulled into a trance.

I opened the cage of my fingers –
a heartbeat, and she was gone.

Kintsugi

When I heard you were knocked
from your bike on Wolfe Tone Quay

I let the teapot slip from my hands
to terracotta kitchen tiles.

A passerby pillowed your head
with his yellow coat, found a photo

of your newborn amongst your things.
I picked up the pottery pieces,

fitted them together with glue,
held the teapot tight. All day I waited

for news, thought of the Japanese masters
who repair precious vessels with seams

of silver and gold. Late in the evening
I found the teapot could not hold.

Sorrel Hill

The last Sunday before Christmas;
clouds hid the hills,

snow melted as it touched the ground.
Bent into the climb, we walked

in twos and threes, taking turns
to carry her, light as she was.

We told stories, funny things
she said and did, memories led us

uphill. Like a cello,
she was tuned to sadness,

happiness came and went,
a chaffinch to her garden gate,

but sorrow stayed
like days of Wicklow rain.

Three hazel saplings
to mark the place we would leave her

among bilberries, bell heather
and ling. A raven played

above us, soaring up
diving down, *kronk*, *kronk*.

There were some words
and a song. Thrown to the sky,

she was lifted by the wind,
blown back to us,

into our hair, our hands,
our eyes.

First Love

In the city's crosscurrents
we meet by chance,

a sudden blush
of sunshine after rain.

We stumble from *you're looking well*
to *how have you been*

while the smell of burnt barley
drifts down the river

and herring gulls reel,
lifting our words like debris

to their nests high above us.
We persist with talk

as if we didn't know the river rises
and falls with the tide,

revealing,
then hiding the walls.

Enclosed

In obedience to the bell I work, eat and pray.
I keep custody of my eyes gladly, strive for silence
in every movement, walk between chapel and cell
with head bent, hands clasped, measured steps.

It was not a passion for Christ that brought me here.
Some days my soul seems bare as the flagstones
in the cloister but there is balm in the daily polishing
of the chapel floor with beeswax and turpentine,

in the way sorrow finds its home among windfalls
in the orchard, in what stirs at dawn when,
as if from the depths of a well, low intoning begins,
collects strength, a long plume of plainsong into the nave.

I have known storms that buffer and batter the heart.
I chose a hard bed, bare boards, a bulwark.

Arctic Hare

When she meets him at family occasions
she grazes his cheek with a kiss;

like a hare on the tundra she senses
when to find shelter, when to change colour.

It's not that she doesn't remember,
not that she doesn't freeze up inside

but she has learned to keep
a wide field of vision,

knows the value of long legs,
light sleep, keen eyes.

Dusk

Do you remember the bell across the river
telling us it's time to walk with sacks

of oats to wooden troughs in the Hill Field,
heave forkfuls over the dung-heap wall,

scatter straw for bedding, feed weanlings
from buckets, stand guard over sucklers

to stop them pucking fostered calves?
Do you remember the voice calling

hup hup hup to the slow chain
of black and white cows, spurts of milk

strained warm into wide, blue-rimmed basins?
Do you remember the scent of wood smoke,

lights coming on in the house, how we longed
for the morning we'd shut the gate and walk away?

On the Boat

(after Julie Otsuka)

On the boat we were mostly virgins,
we talked about who we were going to be –
waitresses, seamstresses, nurses,
we didn't talk about why we had to leave.

We talked about where we were going to be,
the wooden frame house with a picket fence,
but we didn't talk about why we had to leave
as we touched the lockets around our necks.

The wooden frame house with a picket fence
led to talk of lost villages, lost streets
as we touched the lockets around our necks.
We didn't foresee tenements that grew thick as trees

when we talked of lost villages, lost streets
and the diligent men we were going to marry.
We didn't foresee tenements that grew thick as trees,
the suitcase of memories we would have to carry

to the diligent men we were going to marry
when we were waitresses, seamstresses, nurses
nor the suitcase of memories we would have to carry
from the boat, where we were mostly virgins.

Cows at Dugort

Weaving my way
through a New York rush
I think of the herd of cows
at Dugort.

The way they lie
on marram grass,
legs folded elegantly,
heads held high.

The way at low tide
they follow each other
past the lifeguard's hut,
stare out to sea.

The way in the evening
they take to the road,
up the hill by the post office,
heading for home.

Among the Cows

Her father knew where to find her;
she liked to stand among the cows,

they smelled of winter and the dark,
they let her lean into their warm bellies.

She watched them in the fields,
as they moved solid and slow, wrapped

their tongues around sweet grass.
She found her own tune in their lowing,

learned to milk as soon as her hands
were strong enough to squeeze.

When her mother died
her father wore his grief the way

he wore his Sunday suit,
as if it belonged to someone else.

She would listen to the calves
calling for days when weaned,

until their voices, exhausted,
faded like mist from the fields.

The Price

You could fit my father's farm
into two of my husband's fields,
that's why I left, a girl of eighteen,
for the arms of an old man.

Four counties south of the shore
where my mother heaved armfuls
of kelp and carrageen into a creel,
I folded my life into his,

bore him two girls, four boys.
I scrubbed his floors, kneaded his bread,
carried water from his well.
In his wordless way, he was kind

but what price two ponies for a trap,
rooms lit by gas, books on shelves?

Dust Road

To build a road back to him
she had to clear the debris,
briars, stumps and boulders,
level the ground with rake and hoe,

spread crushed stone, their sharp
edges fitting together like puzzles.
She scattered pebbles, no bigger
than wren's eggs, let them settle

in the spaces between,
laid layers of gravel, fines of silt
and clay; a solid foundation
for the weight it must bear.

When she thought it was done
the snow came, stayed for weeks,
left potholes she could dance in,
gravel choking the ditch.

January

The shrunken turlough mirrors
bare trees, frosted fields, a quiet sky.

We fork silage, heave out oats
and barley to curly headed yearlings

in breath-filled sheds. A ewe in-lamb
is stranded on her back.

With a pull to her foot she's up
before jackdaws peck out her eyes.

We talk about the land, the ditches
he dug out in the fifties, gorse bushes

he burned in the sixties, hedgerows
he was paid for in the nineties.

He clambers slow over the gate,
I see his sunken cheeks

and think of other mornings;
herding, reaching up, *carry me Daddy*.

Hands

My father rolls and unrolls the edge
of the sheet, lifts his heavy hands,
looks at them as if they were a stranger's,
drops them back to the white coverlet.

He looks at them as if he has no further use
for them, these hands, scarred by barbed wire,
one finger crooked from when it was crushed
by a rock. He lifts them again, crashes them

to the bed, a wave delivering its cargo to shore,
a weight he can no longer carry.
The monitor above his head bleeps and blinks
to the rhythm of his splintered heart.

The man in the next bed calls through the night,
Ben, come back here Ben, come back.

Winter

Since the trouble with his heart
she tries to keep him in
but before the breakfast tea is cold,
he shrugs on his coat,

lifts his cap, blackthorn stick
and heads out across the fields
to count cattle and sheep,
check how far the flood has risen,

break ice for cows at the pond.
There's not a pick on him,
he feels every breeze like the beech
that shelter Rooney's field

but he will not wear the scarf
or gloves she offers daily.
Back in the kitchen for a fry,
he warms his cheek against hers,

shows her his hands,
thick as fencing stakes, swollen,
purple with the cold. Laughing, he asks
did you ever see such shovels?

Back of an Envelope

I don't know what's come over your father,
my mother says on the phone. He left
a note on the back of an envelope –
gone herding, won't be long.

Where did he think I'd think he was gone?
All those years if I asked where he was going,
where he had been, he'd act like I'd tethered him
to a post, and then today he leaves a note.

Where the River Deepens

Bewildered among pillows, tubes and drips,
she grips my hand with every kick of pain.
I ask if she remembers those days in June,
humming with sunshine and hoverflies
in purple loosestrife when she meets us
at the mill gate on our way home from school.

She carries a basket, heavy with sadness
and buttered scones, bottles of lemonade,
a crochet hook, balls of unravelled wool.
We run through flaggers to where the river
deepens, leap from low branches,
stub our toes on stones, splash and scream.

She watches from the beech-shaded bank, loops
wool through her fingers, closes her eyes for a while.

all I will need

my mother has begun
to number her days

she asks me to choose
from her pieces of silver

as if all I will need
lies polished

beneath a linen cloth
in the sideboard drawer

Every tree

I didn't take the walnut oil,
linseed oil,

the tins of wax
or my lathe and plane

when I closed
the workshop door.

I left the grip of poverty
on the bench

beside my mallet,
whittling knife

and fishtail chisel
with its shallow sweep.

I quit the craft
my father had carved into me

when I was pliable
as fiddleback grain,

left all at the threshold,
except for the scent of wood,

a different scent
for every tree.

Sing

Let choirs make frosty nights sing,
let them tell stories of shepherds

caring for sheep, a stable, a donkey,
a star in the east, while you remember

the road to the church in the woods,
the battened door, timber trusses,

peeling paint and plaster that fell
like snow on the christening font

and harmonium, the pot-bellied
stove that offered a smidgeon of heat,

candlelight soft on the bible
lying open to Isaiah,

For unto us a child is born,
unto us a son is given...

Let yourself sing, diminuendo
or crescendo, as if you still believed.

The River

What surprises me now is not that you're gone
but how I go on without you, as if I'd lost
no more than a finger. My hand still strong,

perhaps stronger, can do what it must,
like carving your name on a branch from the beech
by the Suck, letting the river take you,

so I can call myself free. Only sometimes,
like yesterday or the day before, last night or this morning,
the river flows backwards, uphill to my door.

ACKNOWLEDGEMENTS

Acknowledgements and thanks are due to the editors of the following journals, newspapers, anthologies and websites in which some of these poems have appeared: *The Irish Times, Irish Independent, The Rialto, The North, Poetry Wales, Mslexia, Acumen, Agenda, Ambit, Abridged, The Interpreter's House, Envoi, Southword, The Stinging Fly, Cyphers, The SHOp, The Irish Literary Review, artPapier, Crannóg, The Stony Thursday Book, Tokens for the Foundlings Anthology*, ed. Tony Curtis (Seren Books, 2012), *Anthology for a River*, ed. Teri Murray (River Shannon Protection Alliance, 2012), *The Fish Anthology*, ed. Clem Cairns and Julia Walton (Fish Publishing, 2012), *Listowel Writers' Week Winners Anthology* (Writers' Week Listowel, 2007 & 2014), *The Roscommon Anthology*, ed. Michael & John O'Dea (Roscommon Literary Heritage Group, 2013), *International Baccalaureate Theory of Knowledge Course Companion* (Oxford University Press, 2013), *A Telmetale Bloomnibus*, ed. Clodagh Moynan (Irish Writers Centre, 2013), *The Hippocrates Prize Anthology* (The Hippocrates Press, 2013), *Leaving Certificate Higher Level English Course Papers* (Educate.ie, 2014); https://andotherpoems. wordpress.com/ https://poethead.wordpress.com/ www.dromineer literaryfestival.ie/.

'The River' is displayed in Galway University Hospital. 'Lighthouse Keeper' is displayed in the Hawk's Well Theatre, Sligo.

I wish to gratefully acknowledge a Wicklow County Council arts bursary in 2009.

For their criticism and advice I am grateful to many poetry companions, especially Geraldine Mitchell, Eithne Hand, Jessica Traynor, Liam Thompson, Dominic Tighe, Richard Cox, Yvonne Cullen, Grace Wells, Katie Donovan, Catherine Phil MacCarthy and Airfield Writers. Particular thanks to Shirley McClure and Gillian Clarke. Thanks also to Isobel O'Duffy, Eina McHugh, Mary Ryan, Fran and Dave O'Grady and Christina Mulvey. Finally thanks to my parents, my brothers and all my family and friends for their inspiration, support and encouragement.